MEASURE IT!

DISTANCE, AREA, AND VOLUME

Barbara A. Somervill

www.raintreepublishers.co.uk

Visit our website to find out more information about Raintree books.

To order:

☎ Phone 0845 6044371

🖹 Fax +44 (0) 1865 312263

🖳 Email myorders@raintreepublishers.co.uk

Customers from outside the UK please telephone +44 1865 312262

Raintree is an imprint of Capstone Global Library Limited, a company incorporated in England and Wales having its registered office at 7 Pilgrim Street, London, EC4V 6LB – Registered company number: 6695582

Text © Capstone Global Library Limited
First published in hardback in 2010
Published in paperback in 2011
The moral rights of the proprietor have been asserted.

Edited by Megan Cotugno, Louise Galpine, and Abby Colich
Designed by Richard Parker
Original illustrations © Capstone Global Library Ltd (2010)
Illustrated by Darren Lingard
Picture research by Mica Brancic
Originated by Capstone Global Library Ltd
Printed in China by CTPS

ISBN 978 0 431085 20 3 (hardback)
14 13 12 11 10
10 9 8 7 6 5 4 3 2 1

ISBN 978 0 431085 26 5 (paperback)
15 14 13 12 11
10 9 8 7 6 5 4 3 2 1

British Library Cataloguing in Publication Data
Somervill, Barbara A.
Distance, area, and volume. – (Measure it!)
A full catalogue record for this book is available from the British Library.

Acknowledgements

We would like to thank the following for permission to reproduce photographs: Alamy p. **7** (©Image Source Pink); Corbis p. **18** (TempSport/©Jerome Prevost); Getty Images p. **28** (Stone/GK Hart/Vikki Hart); iStockphoto pp. **12** (rest), **20** (©M. Eric Honeycutt), **23** (©Ufuk ZIVANA), **24** (©Graça Victoria), **25** (©Kriss Russell), **27** (©franklin lugenbeel); Photolibrary pp. **4** (Corbis), **16** (©Pixtal Imaes); Shutterstock pp. **5** (©Racheal Grazias), **11** (©Yulli), **13** (©Zoom Team), **15** (©Erwin Wodicka).

Cover photo of liquid being poured into a beaker reproduced with permission from Shutterstock (©Elemental Imaging).

We would like to thank John Pucek for his invaluable help in the preparation of this book.

Every effort has been made to contact copyright holders of material reproduced in this book. Any omissions will be rectified in subsequent printings if notice is given to the publishers.

Disclaimer

All the Internet addresses (URLs) given in this book were valid at the time of going to press. However, due to the dynamic nature of the Internet, some addresses may have changed, or sites may have changed or ceased to exist since publication. While the author and publisher regret any inconvenience this may cause readers, no responsibility for any such changes can be accepted by either the author or the publisher.

Contents

Some words are printed in bold, **like this**. You can find out what they mean by looking in the glossary on page 30.

What is distance?

Within minutes of your birth, a nurse measured you to see how long you were. The average newborn baby measures 51 centimetres (20 inches) long. Do you know how long you were when you were born? Once you could stand up, your length became height. Doctors measure children to see if they are growing at a normal rate. At ten years old, the average child measures 142 centimetres (56 inches) tall. Are you taller or shorter than average?

Measuring children's growth is one way to see if children are healthy.

Length, height, and distance are all the same type of measurement. They measure the space between one point and another point on a straight line. Sometimes distance measurements must be accurate. The winning pole vault at a track and field event was 5.9 metres (19.4 feet). We use an exact measure to determine the winner. Sometimes, an **estimate** of distance is close enough. The Earth is about 150 million kilometres (93 million miles) from the sun. We do not need to know this measurement to the exact metre.

Measuring distance in the past

Thousands of years ago, people did not have rulers or tape measures. They used body parts as measuring tools. The inch was the width of an adult thumb. A foot was measured as an adult foot. A yard measured from the tip of an adult's nose to the middle finger on an outstretched arm. Longer distances were measured by "pacing" a distance. A pace was the length of an adult man's long step. A field might have measured 80 paces by 110 paces.

Body part measuring was not accurate. Not all adults' arms, thumbs, and feet are the same length. Everyone's measurements were different. People needed something consistent. So they started using **barleycorns**. Three barleycorns laid end-to-end equalled one inch. This was fine for short distances, but it would take thousands of barleycorns and too much time to measure a mile.

This pole-vaulter jumped 5.9 metres to win.

EXPERIMENT!

Try an experiment at home. Choose six small items and put them on a table. Ask an adult to measure each using only hands, feet, or fingers. Record each measurement. Now repeat the measurements using your own hands, feet, and fingers. What did you find out?

The metric system

In the late 1700s, the French were using many different measurement units. In 1790 the National Assembly of France asked the Academy of Sciences to develop **standard** measurement units that were easy to use. The Academy created the International System of Units, which we call the metric system. The unit of distance called the metre was 1/10,000,000 of the distance from the North Pole to the **equator** along the **line of longitude** that passed through Dunkerque, France.

The metre gets its name from the Greek word *metron*, which means "measure". Today, most countries use millimetres, centimetres, metres, and kilometres to measure length. These units are all based on the metre, and all measures in the metric system are based on the number ten.

Metre chart

Unit	Equals ...
1 millimetre (mm)	0.001 metre (m)
1 centimetre (cm)	0.01 metre
1 kilometre (km)	1,000 metres

The metric system is practical for all distance measurements. Millimetres (mm) are perfect for measuring the **diameter** of wire. We measure the length of a newborn baby in centimetres (cm). The length of a building is measured in metres (m). Long distances, like the length from one town to another, are measured in kilometres (km). Metric measurements are easy to use, for short or long distance measurements.

The imperial system

Sometimes people use the imperial system of measurements. This includes inches, feet, yards, and miles. The measurement of a foot comes from the Romans who decided that a foot should be 12 inches. Every nation the Romans conquered – including most of Europe and the Middle East – used a 12-inch foot as a standard measure.

Common US distance units

Unit	Equals ...
1 foot (ft.)	12 inches (in.)
1 yard (yd.)	3 ft.
1 mile (mi.)	1,760 yd. or 5,280 ft.

Converting metric to imperial and imperial to metric

Metric unit	Imperial equivalent	Imperial unit	Metric equivalent
1 millimetre (mm)	0.0394 inches (in.)	1 inch	2.54 cm
1 centimetre (cm)	0.393 inches (in.)	1 foot	30.48 cm
1 metre (m)	1.093 yards (yd.)	1 yard	0.914 m
1 kilometre (km)	0.621 miles (mi.)	1 mile	1.609 km

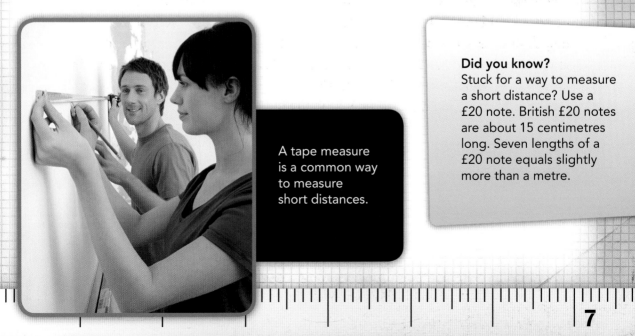

A tape measure is a common way to measure short distances.

Did you know?
Stuck for a way to measure a short distance? Use a £20 note. British £20 notes are about 15 centimetres long. Seven lengths of a £20 note equals slightly more than a metre.

Tools for measuring distance

The tools we use to measure distance depend on the size of the distance. A ruler can measure millimetres and centimetres or inches and feet. A metre stick or a yardstick is fine for the height of a person, but you need a long tape measure for the length of a building. In your car, an **odometer** measures the kilometres or miles you travel.

Measuring very long distances or tall heights can be difficult. Sometimes people use **global positioning systems (GPS)** to measure long distances. GPS calculates distance using computer technology.

Work it out

Max needs to go from Elmdale to Newton. Using a metric ruler, measure the distance from Elmdale to Newton on the map. The scale of this map is 1 centimetre equals 20 kilometres. How far does Max need to travel if he takes the most direct route?

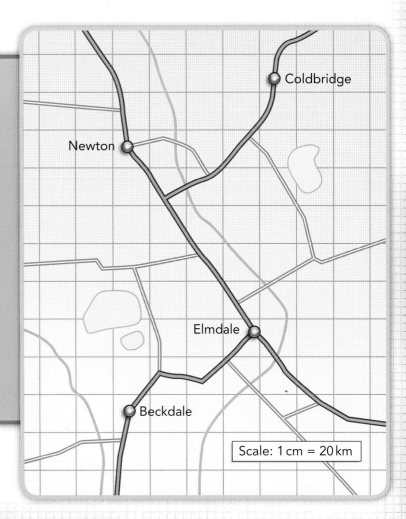

Coldbridge

Newton

Elmdale

Beckdale

Scale: 1 cm = 20 km

Work it out

You can find the height of tall trees and buildings using geometry and **ratios**. The distance from the base point to the woman is 5 metres (A). The distance from the base point to the tree is 50 metres (B). From the base point, the top of the woman's head lines up with the top of the tree. The diagram shows two **right-angled triangles**. The ratio of the woman's height to distance A is the same as the ratio of the tree's height to distance B.

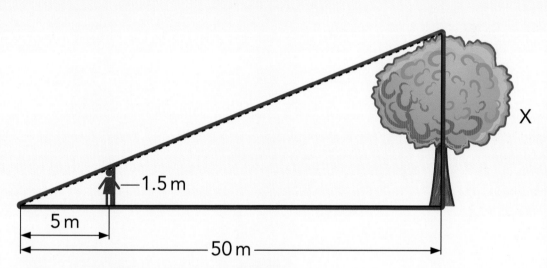

1.5 m is to 5 m as X m is to 50 m.
50 m is 10 times longer than 5 m.
Multiply 1.5 m × 10 to find that the tree is 15 m tall.

What is a great circle?

We're taking a trip from San Francisco, USA, to London. The airline company wants to follow the shortest route to save jet fuel. Of course, they must consider air traffic and storms, but the fastest route around Earth is along a **great circle**.

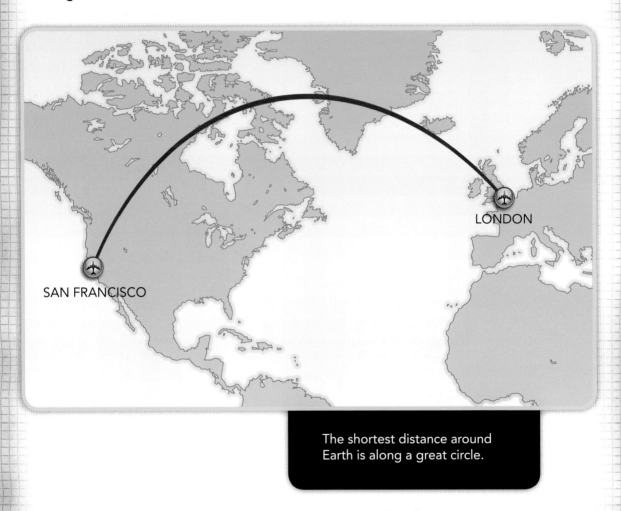

LONDON

SAN FRANCISCO

The shortest distance around Earth is along a great circle.

If you look at a map of the world, you can draw a line from San Francisco to London. The route seems to be a good one, but there is a problem. Earth is not flat like the map. It is more like a **sphere**. We should plan a route based on the shape of Earth, not on a flat map.

A great circle is a circle that runs along the surface of a sphere. If a great circle passed through Earth, it would cut Earth exactly in half. The line it drew would pass through Earth's exact centre. The **equator** is a great circle. **Lines of longitude** are also great circles.

Finding great circles

Several hundred years ago, ship navigators wanted to find fast routes to deliver their cargo to port. The ships travelled the shortest, quickest routes to save time and money. The ships travelled along great circles as much as possible.

Look at a globe. Using your finger, draw a great circle from San Francisco to London. You will find that the shortest route takes you over the North Pole. Continue drawing your great circle. Your great circle that connects San Francisco to London continues on to Rome, Italy, and other places in the world. Travelling the shortest distance saves time, money, and fuel.

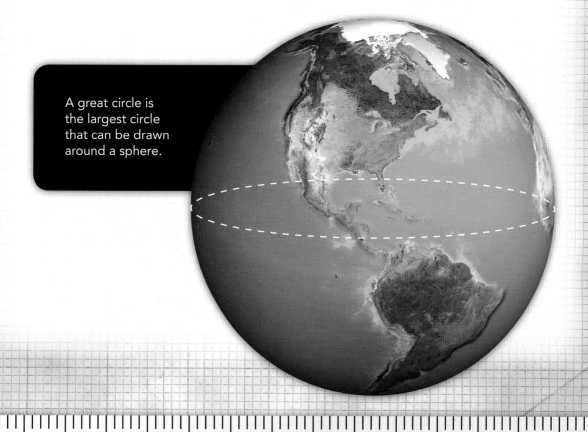

A great circle is the largest circle that can be drawn around a sphere.

What is area?

You can measure the length or height of your desk using a ruler. You can also measure the amount of space taken up the surface of your desk. This is called area. All the space inside a circle is a circle's area. The land or site on which a building stands is the area of the land. Area can be any size or shape. The head of a pin, a farm, and a continent all have area. Area is measured using distance measurements. Length and width are distance measurements. The **radius** and **diameter** of a circle are also distance measurements.

Using area

A golf course's fairways and greens must be mowed every day. The golf course covers 16 hectares (40 acres) of land. The course manager works out that one worker can mow 2 hectares (5 acres) a day. Based on the total area of the course, he needs to hire eight workers for mowing. The manager uses area to develop a work schedule.

Oxen were once used to measure area, but the measurements were not all consistent.

As far back as ancient China, Egypt, and Mesopotamia, land was granted, bought, sold, and farmed according to area. People paid taxes based on the area of land that they owned.

Seed measure always refers to grain crops, never fruit or vegetables.

Area and the metric system

Many countries measure area using the metric system. The metric system uses hectares to measure farmland. One hectare equals 100 metres by 100 metres. The abbreviation for hectares is ha. The area of a city is usually measured in square kilometres, which is written as km^2. For example, Rome, Italy, covers 1,285.3 km^2.

The area of a house or school is measured in square metres. A square metre is one metre by one metre, which is written as m^2. The area of small surfaces, such as tile, is measured in square centimetres. A square centimetre is one centimetre by one centimetre and is written cm^2.

Area and the imperial system

In the imperial system, square inches (sq. in.), square feet (sq. ft.), square yards (sq. yd.), and square miles (sq. mi.) are used to measure area. People use the most convenient units for what they are measuring. For example, a picture might take up 140 sq. in. of wall space. Carpeting a room might require 120 sq. ft. of carpet. A town might cover 14 sq. mi. of land.

Conversion chart

Units for measuring area	Multiply by ...	To get ...
1 acre (ac.)	0.405	0.405 hectares
1 hectare (ha)	2.471	2.471 acres
1 square mile (sq. mi.)	2.6	2.6 square kilometres
1 square kilometre (km^2)	0.386	0.386 square miles
1 square yard (sq. yd.)	0.84	0.84 square metres
1 square metre (m^2)	1.2	1.2 square yards

Knowing surface area is very useful. In the home, measure the area of wall space to plan for wallpaper or paint, or the area of floor space for carpeting. Measure the area of a garden to work out how much grass seed is needed. We buy land for homes or farming by area.

How do you know how much paint to buy? You work out the area of wall space that needs to be covered!

Work it out

A farm owner in Texas donates land to the county for a park. The old **deed** says the land covers 76 sq. mi. The county officials want to know how many km² of land they have to work with. How many km² equals 76 sq. mi.? Use the chart on the left to find out.

What units are used when measuring area?

A clothing company makes hundreds of pairs of jeans every day. The company manager needs to order enough material to make the jeans. How does she know how much material to order? First she arranges the pattern for the jeans on material, being careful not to waste any material. The manager finds that one pair of jeans requires 1.3 m² of material. One hundred pairs of jeans require 130 m² of cloth.

To make a hundred pairs of jeans, manufacturers carefully work out the area of the material they need.

Common area measurement units include metric and imperial units. Metric area measures are all based on the square metre. The most common units used are square centimetres, square metres, square kilometres, and hectares.

Relationship of metric units to the metre

Metric area unit	Relationship to the metre
square centimetre (cm^2)	.01 metre x .01 metre ($0.0001\ m^2$)
square metre (m^2)	1 metre x 1 metre ($1\ m^2$)
hectare (ha)	100 metres x 100 metres ($10,000\ m^2$)
square kilometre (km^2)	1,000 metres x 1,000 metres ($1,000,000\ m^2$)

Sometimes imperial units are used for measuring area. The most common units are square inches, square feet, square yards, square miles, and acres. The chart shows the relationship between these measurement units.

Imperial area measurement units

Unit	Equals ...
1 square foot (sq. ft.)	144 square inches (sq. in.)
1 square yard (sq. yd.)	9 square feet (sq. ft.)
1 acre (ac.)	4,840 square yards (sq. yd.)
1 square mile (sq. mi.)	640 acres (ac.)

Did you know?
Area measurement is expressed in square units, such as square metres or square kilometres. In metric units, the symbol that means square is a small 2 raised above the abbreviation of the unit. It looks like this: $5\ m^2$ or $5\ km^2$.

A **standard** football pitch is rectangular. It can measure 46 to 92 m (150 to 300 ft.) wide by 92 to 119 m (300 to 390 ft.) long. The largest field (92 x 119 m) takes up more than twice as much area as the smaller field (46 x 92 m).

To measure area, we use formulas based on common shapes. The four basic shapes for measuring area are squares, rectangles, triangles, and circles. To find area, use the formula for each shape. Squares and rectangles are easy. Multiply the length by the width. Triangles use the same idea, but they have a different formula. For the area of a triangle, use the formula area equals half of the base (the bottom of the triangle) multiplied by the height.

Here is an example: A triangle measures 4 cm along the base. The height of the triangle is the distance from the base to the highest part of the triangle. If the height of the triangle is 6 cm, then the area of the triangle is ½ of 4 cm times 6 cm, which equals 12 cm^2.

Working out the areas of countries, states, or counties is a bit harder. Few large land areas have straight borders. Most borders follow rivers, coastlines, or major land features. The way to work out the area of any uneven shape is the same for a small garden as it is for a country. Break the area into common shapes: squares, rectangles, circles or parts of circles, and triangles. Work out the area of each smaller shape and then add the area of all the shapes together.

Tools for measuring

We use many of the same tools to measure area as we use to measure distance. Small areas can be measured with a ruler, tape measure, or a measuring stick. Larger areas can be measured using a **distance measuring wheel**. The person measuring the land pushes the distance measuring wheel along the outside border of the land. Today's distance measuring wheels have computers attached and can quickly work out the area of land.

Work it out

Frank wants to plant grass in his garden, but the garden is an odd shape. One bag of grass seed covers 100 m². Work out the area of Frank's garden and decide if he has enough grass seed.

HINT: Divide the shape into 1 rectangle and 2 **right-angled triangles**. Work out the area of each shape and add the areas together.

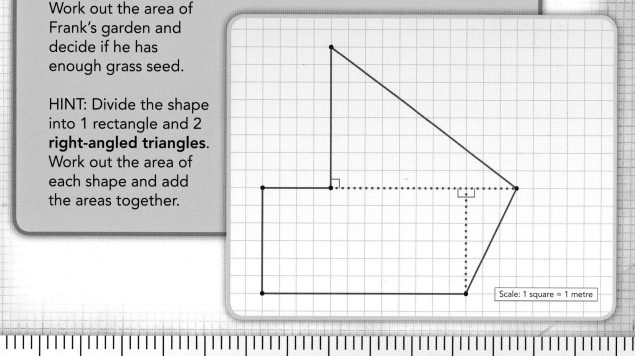

Scale: 1 square = 1 metre

Does our furniture fit?

When you are moving from one home to another or one room to another, there is always one question that needs answering: How will the furniture fit into the room? One way to find the answer is to make a floor plan.

Work out the length of each wall and the total area of the floor.

Here is what you will need to make your floor plan: 2 pieces of graph paper, a tape measure or metre stick, a pencil, scissors, glue, and a compass, if you have any round furniture. Ready? Then, let's begin. Start by measuring the length of each wall in the new room. Write down the measurements and transfer the information onto the graph paper. Allow four squares for every metre. In other words, for a wall that measures 4 metres, draw a line 16 squares long. When you have all the walls drawn on your plan, measure and mark the doorways and cupboards.

Next, measure each piece of furniture going in the room. Draw the shape of each furniture piece on graph paper, using the same scale as your floor plan: one square on the paper equals 25 centimetres in your room. Label each furniture piece and cut the shapes out. Place the shapes on your floor plan and move them around until they fit in the room. Make sure there is still room to open the door! When the plan is finished, glue the furniture shapes onto the plan. You can use it as a guide when arranging your furniture.

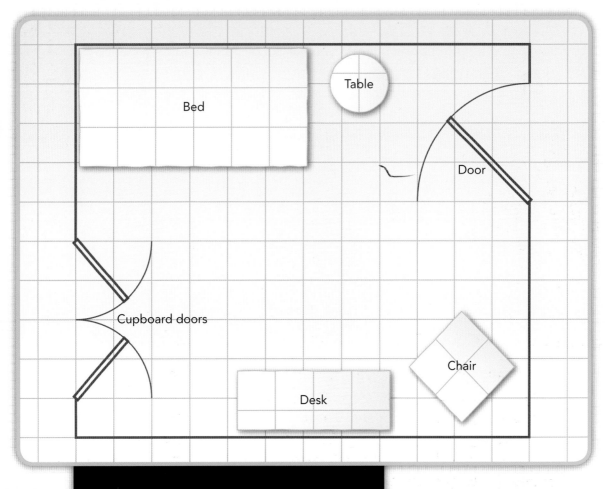

Draw a diagram of the room and all the furniture to scale on graph paper. Cut out the furniture pieces and place them in the room's space.

What is volume?

Volume and capacity are two ways to measure the size of three-dimensional objects. Volume refers to how much space an object takes up. To find volume or capacity, we use distance measurements. A plastic container measures 10 centimetres long, 5 centimetres wide, and 20 centimetres high. To find the volume of the container, multiply the three measurements together. The volume of the container is 1,000 cubic centimetres (cm^3). Volume can also mean the amount a container holds, such as a litre, a gallon, or a teaspoon.

What is capacity?

Capacity is slightly different from volume. Capacity measures the amount an object holds. Drivers have to fill up their cars with fuel. The amount of fuel each fuel tank holds is the tank's capacity. The capacity of the average small car's fuel tank is about 49 litres (13 gallons).

Work it out

Chris offered to make punch for a class party. His recipe only serves 8 people, but there are 24 in his class, including his teacher. Here are the ingredients from the recipe he plans to use:

250 ml cranberry juice   175 ml apple juice
325 ml ginger ale   125 ml raspberry sorbet

To make enough punch for the class, Chris must multiply the volume of each ingredient by 3. How much of each ingredient does he need?

Eggs are ellipsoid or ovoid shapes. Every egg is slightly different in size, so each has a slightly different volume.

Solid shapes have volume. The most common solid shapes are cones, cylinders, cubes, rectangular solids, and **spheres**. There are also ellipsoids shaped like eggs, tetrahedrons shaped like pyramids, and several other solid shapes. These solids have three dimensions. Depending on the shape, most solids have length, width, and height. Spheres are "solid circles", and their measurements depend on the **radius** of the circle and **pi (π)**, which equals approximately 3.142. Pi is a number that is used when measuring circles. This includes solid round shapes, such as spheres, egg shapes, cones, or cylinders.

Using capacity and volume

Capacity measures how much a container holds when it is filled to the top. It is the ability of a container to hold, receive, or absorb substances. A glass holds liquid. Soil holds rainwater, and a sponge absorbs liquid. Glasses, soil, and sponges have capacity.

Volume is used every day in cooking, packaging, and shipping. Businesses want to use the best shape and size when packaging a product. They must label most food products according to either volume or weight. Shipping across a city or across an ocean also uses volume. Shippers need to work out how much of their product will fit into a shipping container.

When baking, we usually measure liquid ingredients by volume. This container measures cups, ounces, litres, and millilitres.

What units are used when measuring volume?

If a hot air balloon is filled with air, why does it rise? The answer is that a volume of hot air weighs less than the same volume of cold air. One cubic metre (35 cubic feet) of air heated to 38°C (100°F) weighs about 250 grams (9 ounces) less than the same volume of cold air. Each cubic metre of heated air lifts 250 grams (9 ounces) of weight, which explains why hot air balloons are so big. A balloon needs a huge volume of hot air to lift the balloon, basket, and passengers.

If there is not a large enough volume of heated air in a hot air balloon, the balloon will not fly.

In the metric system, we measure volume by cubic centimetres (cm³) and cubic metres (m³). Car engines are measured in cubic centimetres. Garden mulch, topsoil, and concrete are measured in cubic metres. **Capacity** is measured in millilitres (ml) and litres (l). When baking, vanilla and milk are measured in millilitres. The capacity of a large soft drink bottle is 2 litres.

In your home, you use volume and capacity measurements all the time. You may have containers in the kitchen for storing flour, sugar, coffee, and tea. You have baking dishes, pots, and pans that hold different amounts of food for cooking.

Sometimes imperial measurement units are used for measuring volume and capacity. Volume is measured is cubic inches (cu. in.), cubic feet (cu. ft.), and cubic yards (cu. yd.). You might measure a box of chocolates in cubic inches, a refrigerator in cubic feet, and cement in cubic yards. Common capacity measurements include pints and gallons. You might buy a pint of milk or a gallon of petrol.

Metric to imperial conversion chart

Metric to imperial	Imperial to metric
10 ml = 2 teaspoons	1 teaspoon = 5 ml
10 ml = 2/3 tablespoon	1 tablespoon = 15 ml
500 ml = 2.1 cups	1 cup = 237 ml
500 ml = 16.9 fluid ounces	1 fluid ounce = 30 ml
1 l = 2.1 pints	1 pint = 0.47 l
1 l = 0.26 gallon	1 gallon = 3.8 l

Cooks and bakers often measure ingredients in special containers. These include teaspoons (tsp) and tablespoons (tbsp). These tools measure salt, flour, and other ingredients. In the United States, cooks use cups for measuring some ingredients.

Did you know?
Volume measurement is expressed in cubic units, such as cubic metres or cubic centimetres. In the metric system, the symbol that means cubic is a small 3 raised above the abbreviation of the units. It looks like this: 5 m^3 or 5 cm^3.